What Remains
and
What Disappears

Poems by

Francis L. Richardson

What Remains and What Disappears

Published by 11thour Press
www.11thourpress.com
Printed in the United States of America
ISBN: 978-154297579-7

Cover art: Joseph R. Lombardo

Acknowledgments:
First and foremost, to Steve Abbott, without whose supervisory editorial and production skills this book could not have taken place, profound thanks for his manifold helps and kindnesses; and to my wife Kathleen, whose help and encouragement were indispensable. Many thanks also to Joseph R. Lombardo, who designed the book's beautiful cover and to the following publications in which certain of these poems appeared:

Cap City Poets (Pudding House, 2008): "Recognizing"
Cider Press Review: "August Morning Song"
High Plains Literary Review: "Magic"
In the Arts: "Cima da Conegliano"
Larry's Poetry Review No. 4: "Absence"
The Minnesota Review: "Bachus and Philemon"
The New Yorker: "Country Couple"
The Smith: "New England Aristotelian"

Walking (chapbook, Pudding House 2007): "Grandmother", "Over Easy", "Walking to Thee", "The Ghost", "Ohio (Confessional Poem)", "Today", "Country Couple", "The Wereman", "Two Paintings by Goya", "If You Had Known", "The Color of Your Money: a Story", "Menaces to Society and the Planet", "Family Photographs", "Magic", "Pouring a Child's Glass of Milk", and "Hidden Costs"

11 th🕐ur Press

To my mother,
who first introduced me to poetry

Table of Contents

I

Recognizing

Walking past, walking among
the dying, newly coined elms, my sight
overlaid with panes of experience like
isinglass, like semi-transparent
cataracts I see how every spring
the world grows younger
and younger yet—flesh
and satiny leaf and sun—globed
within the sky's
soft unfocused blue
eye.

Only we, I and the people I know
grow older, gradually enter
another and less instantaneous
kind of being.
The body's shapely, animate hourglass
becomes the turnip watch
and we keep time
in a different way
recognizing that similes last longer
than what they describe
and that people were made not to be seen
but to be used.
There is the sleep of water
in a pitcher with sun slanting through it
and the sleep of fruit
with the sun stored inside it

And I think of someone I knew, who
when she began, late spring of 1872,
came into a world that had been there
forever, on all things fabulously
and securely old.
Spring by spring that world grew younger
to include, presently, her children

and afterwards theirs—always younger, and dearer,
and less easy to understand, until one morning
as the pear tree in her back yard was putting on white
for the eightieth time, her world became too new
to be borne, and slipped into unbirth.

I begin to understand
what before I would not bear to know:
how it happened.

Embarkation for Cythera

All the long gracious morning melodious sirens
Welcomed our going; streamers floated and spun
Between us and the crowd on the dock as they called,
        fluttered, wished
And we waved back without knowing quite why
Or how long. But below decks the parties unravelled,
The last to go went, warned by spreading thrums from
        the engines;
The metal blast of the horn erased all lighter farewells;
Then widening water soon undistinguished the faces
Until they or we turned away.

And now, the time-emptied sea hours
That pass as the sea that we watch washing past,
The hard, brilliant, marvelous dark blue
Of water that's carven and changes
All slipping beyond and away.
And of course there are meals, games, the bar,
Movies, dances, the rooms and the music, each like all;
And we two, relaxing in deck chairs,
Always closer and more unfamiliar
As days wheel overhead, and nights—
Clocks set back (or ahead) in the mornings—
And this vast ship crawls steadily forward
Through gentling winds and beneath a more searching sun
To the island below our horizon, presumably Southern
Of weather, its snow-peaks still hidden in clouds,
From which, it is rumored, no one
Returns the same.

Icarus Ascending

Sheer and sheer up
am-
ong soundless heights of wind
and light
towers of air without walls
cliffs of light without summit
I divide the high from the deep
and they are equal.
Blue forever on up
islands of cloud below
and below them
sunny blue
motionless and limitless
summers of blue

Summer and winter, fall and
spring
I leave your realms behind
like a turtle entering
the transparent cave of myself
o burning world
o summer
as I rise

The Passion

A large, wild park at the center of my gridiron city:
How large and how wild it was I did not know until I went in
and was lost.
Glint-whetted grass, brisk
trees, the air is stronger and colder, almost pure oxygen,
like breathing cider, but in it almost anything
may catch quick fire and burn white burn burn
burn without stopping, and what does not burn
rusts.

It's always there, but I do not go there
again, for me no more that timeless day
of thunder crackling in the blue sky,
not again that moment when everything
is suddenly clear, and bright,
and I turn to hit you.

When I had found my way out I slept
I don't know how long.
Perhaps forever.

Grandmother

I will remember you back out of the grave
Into which nobody saw you go anyway—it could have been empty
That closed box that slid into the pit in
Some immense cemetery that sprawled out over three cindery hills
    in Philadelphia
No one now remembers where, nor its name even—
    I could never find that grave again—
It overlooked a railroad track—
And I am the only one still alive that saw it happen.
And I deny it.

I will remember you back into a day like today,
Though it's not today, I will regather
The austere freshness of your faint perfumes
Which while I live will never be wholly dispersed.

Do you hear that snarling train-horn? its harsh reiterated
    nyah-nyah?
That's me, calling you through the nights
Not with the soft, mild voice of my grownup years
But with the rage and grief of the fierce child
I was and you knew and you loved. You hear me. And I hear
You, your laugh even in somebody else's voice,
Your boiler-explosion sneeze, your funny
Gay Nineties songs that you mostly forgot half the words of,
But the tune was right.
Never mind if there are no words yet, they'll be along later.
We've got the tune.

And so,
I will remember you back, out of the grave,
Out of that stupid grave and into the days
Of the world still to come.

Geezers

We rely on memory
of tunes past
since today's music
has no tunes
(to speak of).

Time overtook us
on the road, which became
the interstate. We had
to move over
to the slow lane.

Above us glow and wheel
the same old constellations.
Some times we're tempted
to say, River,
river of stars,
take all.

We had not realized
we were characters in a book
written by someone else,
an author we had not read, or
heard of.

Adieu

When I kissed my sweetie, I ate her, her lipstick,
cigarettes, Scotch, Beech-nut gum, the Albany Times-
Union, the New York Central train whistle, country
roadhouses, the Battle of Stone Arabia

I became the Mohawk River, chewing away at all
these things plus sandstone and limestone

When she kissed me, I never knew what she tasted
or what she swallowed or what river she became
(the Podunk? the Galiano?)
But it was not the river she wished to be,
nor is the Mohawk the river I was best at
becoming.

Over Easy

I don't want to make too much of this, but—
A wisp of smoke sidewinds upward
From the black shine
A whiff of olive oil says
Hot enough

I crack (crunching click) the shell
On the cast-iron rim
And things start to spoing and sputter.

For me it's easy
With the ease of long practice,
No thought required

But if I do think, suddenly I'm
Awash in significance, swept off my routine feet
By the force, the wave-weight of all that work and thought
That enables this humdrum sacrament.
The labor it took, and takes
To intercept the chicken's wild life-cycle,
To channel the life-force of silver, twisted trees,
To capture and reshape old outcrops of
A planet's molten core.
Geez!
People doing this all the time
Since before history
And I haven't even started on the toast!

So I shout
"How d'ya want em?"
And the answer floats down,
"Over easy"

The Traveler

I thought of the mountains, but we were passing through
      the cornfields;
The light sparkled like water on the long leaves of the corn.
A crow flew westering over. This afternoon.
Tonight I lie on the narrow back of sleep
In my slant room with a washbasin
And listen to them laughing and then
Gasping in the next room. Tonight
I had to be helped up the stairs.
I am a Dutchman but I speak perfect English.
I have often been told so. I learned it
In San Francisco, where I lived five years
As a boy. I am single. Though I am a Dutchman,
I thought of the mountains.
I knew that crow.

A Glass

Transparent snow on snow
shines in that unfilled glass, the mellow glitter of it
darkening now around the wine
as the host pours.

Snow falling early this year, falling this afternoon
on the red and yellow leaves, topping them
with a quaint crust like icing,
the colors showing still
through and between.

Snow falling in the deep midwinter's dark grey afternoon
when I was nine—sledding tomorrow!—
snowing so fast, would it get higher than me?—
me, brimming with awe, delight, dread—

Now that thirst
to drink again
as one had drunk in youth

Fragile, but not knowing it
yet, a brilliant curve that
will need to be filled, become translucent to
light living in not just itself, or air,
but in the dark
wine of now
and of then known
in the light of now.

I didn't then
know what I was drinking.

Melting snow. Time. Thirst.
And the vessel, the light, and the wine
becoming commingled, confused. Which of these
is I? All of them?

Snow on transparent snow
shines in that glass.

Black Dog Sings Blues

Not baby blue.
Not a blue-skies-smiling-at-you sky blue,
more a corroded blue,
not the blue of delphiniums (or if you insist delphinia),
more like the black-blue of dolphinia;
a blue like the sound of a car engine not starting
or non-starting, not now, not ever, an obstinate, hopeless,
        vindictive blue.
Get it? Earth's natural beauty is not in the picture.
A puddle mixed of mud, sludge, rust, gunpowder, rainwater,
        engine oil
blue reflecting a black sky or no sky and adding a particularly
evil iridescence to it. That blue.

Or if you wish to fly dead
into the wind of ancient wisdom
as no mere bluebird (twittering nitwits!) ever did or would,
let's hear it for the classic
black-blue of Medea's hair and/or
the paralytic blue of Medusa's splintery eyes, each glance
        a syringe of
snake venom driven into your nerve-centers – snake-eyes
smiling at you -- and/or
the blue of Lady Macbeth's cold hands in the middle of the night,
cold hands, cold heart.
My kind of girl. And,
My kind of blue.
How about you?

Group Portrait

What is a solid? My solid aunt
inhabits illusion. Not hard,
impenetrable, she lives in the written world.

My mechanical aunt, sitting over against us,
is made of non-rigid materials, cannot be grasped
by the human hand.

Watch: she balloons
in her chair, then dwindles
to a metaphysical point. She's an expert dwindler.
She goes to some lengths not
to appear God-made; carefully polished,
no trace of the artist's hand remains upon her.

She has no subsequent history.
No vicissitudes. No sunstorms
disrupt her circuits, trouble her grids.

It is in fact to prevent this kind of occurrence that
the inside of her skull is wallpapered
in flowered asbestos.

But she is a fragile system, and though her glories
are not precisely mortal
they depreciate.

Walking to Thee

Walking to thee—
still a long way this side of the river
which I cannot see
but its great gouge splitting the country
in two, that I see
and the land on the other side, flowing back
under a pale sky forever, its long plains,
its bluish hills made tiny by distance—

How shall I cross?
I know that river is large and tremendously steep,
one could toss down it forever.
I am getting older, and I was never
a long swimmer. Loss
and the fear of loss lighten my bones, lighten
my head. Of bridges and boats here
I have heard nothing. I think
there aren't any.

Perhaps I can do it
only by walking backward
—walking backward while looking forward, it's
only a few steps back
to where thou standest with thy
camera, taking a picture of all this country:
a picture that includes me.

Winter, Northern Arizona

The white grass that beckons outward from the roadside
over cindery ground, like thin hair blond as snow pulled
flickering constant with the constant wind, always away
towards the frail window at the distant rim, a window
without glass through which sky gleams
and beckons again.
The window opens through my rib-cage.
The road runs on.

The Place

The Queen of Spain said to my sister Alice
(An ex-queen, really; dead these six hundred seasons)
"Alice," she said, "I like you so much, you must come
        and see me.
We'll laugh at the dwarfs and whisper through
        the court entertainments,
Meet on the iron pathways of the implacable dances,
And on winter afternoons we'll embroider -- talk and stitch,
Stitch and talk until fingers and lives slow, stiffen
To part of the pattern in the cold.
You won't like the palace, it's badly lit
And very comfortless, but at the back stretch out
The barren gardens of memory where we shall walk
Diminished; there nothing changes.
You'll come, won't you? You'll stay for a long visit."

Alice, a lovely person, her trouble was always
She couldn't say no.
She went to the dark, cramped, tortuous palace.
We've lost the way out.

The Ghost

Not more than
the damp that comes through
the plaster wall, that discolors it slightly
a sense of subtle disorder
among the canisters
deja vu
A household smell
mixed and elusive, inseparable
The presence
like a not very strong
memory from a journey,
memory that will not last long--
The cast-iron bandstand and the leafless
horse-chestnuts, a little gate that swung
without a latch
and the gravel that exhaled dust.

Your impression on the air
anxious, dutiful daughter, then wife
who tried hard to keep up
with her life
couldn't
now is nobody's daughter
nobody's bride, housekeeper, wife.

Old Orchard

Old shoes, dirt road, an almost
Obliterated path
Leading into, moving on into
Baleful old tangled orchards, low
Scaly branches, spikes,
A few gnarled apples
Here and there – bite,
Avoid the worm-holes, a taste
None could describe:
Gritty-acrid-sweet, earthy, yes
But that only begins it.
A taste from former times, the tree
Begun long before
You were born. Or I.
Winter and sorrow.
Winters and sorrows survived
And long since gone.
Yet here they still are
Englobed, the tough skin, warty and spotted,
Beneath which, still,
The flesh.

What Remains and What Disappears

Someone is walking ahead of me
not far, but not clear
dimmed by the intervening
fall of snow, like a figure on a thin
old coin, its relief worn so down
it is almost not there.
It seems strange, someone
out walking naked in the snow.
How far can he go?

He was never found.
Not even after, when the thaw
unburied the brown earth.
As if his body were water, and had drowned
into the ground.

How can anyone ask, where
are the snows of yesteryear?
They are right here.
These are they, through which I
indistinctly see
him ahead of me --
grayly falling, falling,

II

Waking From Dream, Maybe

To have been running
or walking, breaking into a run
from under the dust-colored turmoil
of thundercloud as the first drops hit,
running with others in a shuffle of voices—

Then at one jump, at one bite engulfed by
the towering blue maw
of the real day, that mouth
edged at intervals by glittering chips of tooth
diguised as dwellings. To be standing
on its delicately undulant blue-black tongue.
The roof of that mouth ridged with silvery cloud.

So this is Columbus, Ohio!
What an unbelievably usual place.
Can this really have been, all along,
life's secret
destination?

Here

As I walk up the long street I watch the sky
losing light; its fizzy jet streams turn
an absurd but tender pink. Wet
leaves muffle the sidewalks,
branches show like wires; the grass
is still bright (darkening) green.

Sometimes this humdrum world, this sky,
are unsufferably beautiful, but tonight not.
As light removes, as the doors
of possibilities slam shut
in the wind of time,
the cosmic bubble seems to shrink
to a manageable size.
Columbus, Ohio.

Yet only seems.
For everything is really more remote
than I'd ever realized, more unknowable.
Farther apart.
And the years I spend here,
walking up this street, are years
I cannot be anywhere else, find
anywhere else, know
anywhere else. And also
the years I spent elsewhere were years
I could not be here.

Ohio (Confessional Poem)

I haven't always lived here.
But

That other kind of witness
I have refused, and refuse,
To bear. I will not.

I'm not a wilderness
Any more, I moved to Ohio and became,
Rather, a countryside—unmemorable,
Kind, useful, something I very deeply
Wished to be.

Ohio: a state
Largely unknown because
So terribly familiar.

I admit I miss the purposeless wildness, the
Hurricane gusts in which I roared
And thrashed and my forests
Were torn apart. Hurricanes don't
Arrive in Ohio, and if they did,
They'd ruin the crops.

Ohio: the marvel and terror of life
Abounds in a pasture. a woodlot.
A mini-mall.

Let's face it: we live here.
I'll sing it.

The Scarecrow

At the end of the path that leads up between the fields,
just where it opens out into the widest field of all,
a tatterdemalion scarecrow
burns forever.

A disgusting object—man shaped,
so old, so grimy, so pitiful—
blond flame springing from its hung head,
its smiling mouth if you get close enough

The flames that gush out and up
from between its non-existent ribs, that
spiral round its stick arms,
flap colorless white against the day skies,
yellow-white into the black night skies.
Rain or shine makes no difference.
There is almost no smoke.

I don't live out there, haven't
since I was a kid.
I guess you would call us suburbanites. But
some frosty nights when the leaves are gone
on the way home from a party maybe,
I see it. It looks like a yellow star.
And in the quiet
you can hear the tinny crackling clear down here.

How could I have forgot?

Listening at Sunset

You've slowed my heart
So that I can die
Some day now.

I listen at sunset
To the bird at the river's bank
Its one-note call.

Silence, then it comes again;
Only one note, but its voice
Like an oboe.

No more the fierce bagpipes
That would suddenly transform me.

That was in the days before
I knew what would happen,
And how small was my power
To make it be different.

Self Portrait at 83?

This man is my umbrella.

Its iron ribs; its frayed fabric; its
Dark dome shape all
Rusty, but
Trusty.
If long outmoded.

However, once it's
Gone, the iron
Cage shattered, the fabric rotted, and
With nothing left to protect ---

Who will remember?
What I remembered?

Today

The sky today: blue
unshuttered beyond,
the crystal dome of nothing
visible, the same forever
but today unshuttered

We drove
over the bronzing farmlands
past the silver-gilt standing ghosts
of the corn, tall, frail,
and gentle in this light,
to walk in a graveyard that climbed
a slow hill, then descended the other side.

My wife, little son, and I among
so many lives, so many symbols—
dandelions' perfect globes of cottony stars, galaxies
before the dispersion,
the black velvet swallowtail flourishing his blue and gold
teardrops,
the named, white, rectangular stones shaped like closed
books,
the vast book of all things visible and invisible
its crystal leaves open
to today.

"Sacred," sang the kernel, the yellow stone box
with spiral columns rising at the four corners
"Sacred to the memory of Valentine Reber
and his wife, Magdalena" born
far away, two hundred years ago,
but here now
here now
forever.
Their children and their children's children lie
at anchor in concentric widening rings

within this grass-green slow-descending wave, Ohio clay,
around that central, spiral-columned stone.

"Sacred," speaks the tree, the very old cedar
beside it, Sacred
to memory and more than memory it rises
in lasting green-black fire.
Its bark speaks in contours
pearly and reddish like sand
combed into long, purposeful
strands—flows down, flows up
unbroken, smooth but not straight, encompassing
accidents, prophesies eternity unscrolling
perfect as water
or the whorls of a child's hair.

III

August Morning Song

Still,
August is almost morning.
August morning sun is hot lemon sherbet
fragrant in the sky;
lights me up.

Venti soffici—featherbed winds
drift in through the windows
and stay awhile.
No refrain,
but happy chance—
happenstance
an access to perfection?
It's not the usual.

The four-cornered, fern-covered
bedspread of earth is
late again; I'll lie instead
on pillowy air.
Let me try. Hereafter's a short fall;
Abide, abode.
See? As simple as that.

Consider the rights of noon.

December Morning Song

Sky streams on overhead
a universal concatenation
of blackboard erasers
Television aerials rock stiffly
The windows buffle
as the warm gale flows through England
Oh joyful and thankful I
to be in that strong flow, that dark succession.

The navy-blue flag stands out straight from its pole
ridges running through it as across sea-water
so fast they hold it still
still as a compass needle
is held still

Pigeons skate down the air diagonally, out of control,
heading for smash, their smooth semicircles pulled
past shape like invisible taffy
ravelling beyond
horizon

Bird-flight, cloud-threads, flag-fall, all
combed out, pulled straight, held still
in flowing.
Oh joyful and thankful I
to be held I too, I too, in that vast direction.

Elizabeth Angel

Elizabeth angel
look at the sky clipped into silver paper-patterns
by the cutleaves (angular angels' wings)
of the cutleaf maple: clip clip clip clip
and the sky flutters down around us
as weightless fragments like darkening
snowflakes, like shards
of monochrome kaleidoscope.

The light tarnishes, as today
moves away from us westward.
Silver paper turns black paper.
Nothing will tarnish the cylinder of light
on which we lie,
two kaleidoscope bits that fit
together.

Joy in Autumn

Joy! Joy in the pale red brick doorway,
An entrance,
Joy in the cool noon light;
Joy in the dead leaf,
Its crisp ridges and diverging estuaries
Beginning to crumple,
A russet topographical map
Beginning to fade
As the memory of a departed life
Ebbs from it;
Joy in the iron-grey rough-barked tree
Almost divested; free
To comb out the wind unencumbered,
Letting in the light, free
To sleep, its structure fully in view,
Coming back to the beginning.
There is an afterward
Which will, perhaps, be like before.

And there is now.

Country Couple

They return in my thoughts with something woody
    in their kind
Gestures and faces, almost as semi-
trees of unequal height but like shape,
Both knurled and sparse and knobby
From growing in a thin soil, a brusque climate;
One pinkish, the other silver-gray-skinned.

Around them there were always gardens, all kinds of
    gardens.
On the north juniper, on the south grapevines;
Crimson roses, orange zinnias, apple trees
Full of green apples; a big stone-walled square plot
Bristling with pole beans and sweet corn.
Their house grew too, unfurled like a pumpkin vine
Over the rocky ledge where it had found a hold
Two hundred weathered years before them.

When they became too old, it outgrew them,
And they moved to three little rooms in town.
But they still had a garden, a small
Weeping willow that, as we drank iced tea
One endless afternoon,
Pored over us, traipsed its strands of weed
Slowly across our faces, spelled us
Captive where we sat in reclining chairs.

New England Aristotelian

Hammer down the boards, the bars of bell song;
Shut the shutters of leaf light;
Close the stone-colored door.
This world, which was everything to him,
Has no shape for him any more.

He lived to know, yet now
Unknowing he lives on
In the vegetable mews
Deaf in the apple tree, close in the green, hard
apples that grow harder, smaller
Year by year, day by day—waning
green moons.

Eventually the ladyslippers
Live one by one, privately,
Hiding, or merely keeping to themselves,
The threadlike veins
In their delicate pink jowls .
Flesh blooms in the woods.

The Wereman

The one I invoked
always, the one who stands
between
me and you
is absent

There is no glass in the
windows
its tutelary glitter is absent
night and wind pour through
the rooms

Then the black dog who
turns
in the night into a white-
skinned black-haired
man. A black dog with a
white stripe down his chest

The planet rusts
between suns

receding
tiny
past
explosions
of light

Starlight
When did I change?

No Man's Land

Beyond the sheer plate glass, five miles ago
The island sits, low, compact, blue.
No more. Beyond again
The light blue mountains of the shore retreat
Into the farther past, their upper walls
Still faintly dusted and seamed with snow.
Dark brilliant the sea.
Behind me he,
White on his white bed,
Stirred drily, said
"All the people I used to know have turned against me."

IV

Cima da Conegliano
(c.1460-1519)

You looked
at the boards mortised together in the shape
of a round-topped door, and you sealed that door
shut, covered it with smooth plaster
and the plaster with ground-up semi-precious
stones floated in oil, polished those stones
as you knew how, to make the door
become a mirror
to reflect not you exactly
but the world that looked out of your eyes: the world
before you grew up in it.

The world awakening
at the end of your side street in Conegliano
or just beyond, awakening with your senses—
its castles sparkling matter-of-factly
against the resurrected blue, its country saints
struck into wood by the astonishment of being,
the thought that comes on them,
the impulse of adoration too strong
to know how to obey.
In such a moment what
can even a saint do?

That same morning, in the rocky orchard
back of Aunt Nicolosia's
there is Daniel, wringing his hands and peering
anxiously upward, too nervous to notice
that the lions, in their standoffish way,
look friendly. And farther on, beyond
the Collalto gate, a mile or so outside town,
David and Jonathan are walking home together.
They are both about ten years old; David
carries a sword too big for him and also Goliath's head
and he is telling Jonathan all about how it was.

You knew
that open doors conduce to disappearance
but you no more than anyone else
could seal all the doors.
You disappeared.
So did the world.
But the mirrors you made
still reflect that strong early moment
you wanted to keep, and kept.

Leonardo Knew

Leonardo knew
that almost everything is vicious;
though he dreamed otherwise
and drew, sometimes, his dreams.

But he saw clearly
the clear eyes willing death
clear as water, clear as ice, clear
as glass, the eyes
burning into his own. Returning
his glare.

He saw the terrible abyss, falling away within
the beautiful face. The cheekbones pitiless cliffs
round which crows swing.

Today too
the intensity of vice
is what's hard to believe,
to predict, and to falsify—the strength
of the will to eat
your brother, the strength that grinds
his bones, his living
bones to make your bread.
Enriched bread.

Old man, remote in your age and your greatness
as the uninhabited mountains that stretch back behind Mona Lisa,
behind St. Anne, behind grandmother, mother, child, tree, lamb—
you foresaw, near the end of your life,
the end of the world
as vortical dust.
And nothing you saw was unrelated.
Does the lens
need to be finer still?
Is there another way
to look at this?

A Venetian Annunciation

after Titian's masterpiece
in the church of San Salvador in Venice

The gesture is of
Recognition, as the light catches
The edge of her hand.
This woman is different, and the difference:
She always knew it would happen.

Details were unforeseen—
The soundless turmoil of angels threshing above her,
Their silver skins like fish; the white bird
Riding implacably down its pathway of light
Growing, growing until it became
That enormous winged thing on the ground beside her—
The how was peculiar and frightening, but
Even while it began she knew
That it was what it was.
The light dancing on the underside
Of low bridges, the calling of cats
Lonely in a stone universe had long ago told her,
So that when the walls of her room fell away
And the sky turned reddish-brown
And the trees gusted into black fire
She rose quickly and surely and lifted her veil.

Who as a child had sung
"There would I be,
High among chiming birds in Jesse's twisted tree."

Two Paintings by Goya
(The Family of Charles IV; the 3rd of May)

Who are these people?

Don't they know what time it is?
Twinkling and sparkling like the low
Sun off the oncoming water
By virtue of their diamonds, their
Medals, slick fabrics, gold sword-hilts, decorations

While just outside town people are being shot
By the score. The future is now.
The dark, cold, shut town
Sitting there like a disconsolate offshore rock
Beyond
Just beyond
Where the people and the guns intersect
In the bloody sprawl that goes on and on.

They didn't see anything coming.
They never knew what hit them.

It simply didn't occur to them
That somebody had to pay for all this—
That things have to be paid for

Not necessarily by the people who own them
Or by those they love
If they love anybody.

Red, all that slick red, white,
And black.
And the rushing, sparkling water
Coming in fast.

A tide of diamonds—hard, material stars.

Goya's Still Lifes

Can there be
good faith? in
dead birds, fish on a table
flopping or bent wide-eyed
harshly stiffening
corpse-heads
stacked

stacked again

or in
the sinister crust of sugar
on the donut, the blackness
of grapes, things
to be eaten.

But oh
how beautiful
the spindling legs
of the dead russet birds,
their trivial ineffable
softness, their
lustre fading as we look

as darkness falls.

Max Ernst: Children Threatened by the Song
of a Nightingale

Max, you were right, nightingales
can appall; and you listened. Your ear for danger saved you—
while millions who didn't want to hear anything
died.

Over and over.

Children , you
are right to flee
that throaty note
fluttering and faltering among the fireflies,
trying to sing an unspeakable story
out of a past that is not yours—
but it soon may be yours—

A story
that could happen again, tonight, as the stars
swing overhead in the same patterns,
while the mute chorus of fireflies blinks and jitters
a warning that cannot be heard—
could happen tonight
to you.

For you play a part
in a dream not dreamt by you
—Who is that dreamer? Your father?
your neighbor? your mother? your Commander-in-Chief?—a part,
            of whose requirements you had no idea
when you auditioned; did you know
you auditioned?
Your name up in lights:
It can be arranged: your part may demand
that your agony be transfixed
in nail-points of light against the black, void sky
eternally coming around again
with the nights and the seasons

as a warning, an emblem, a frozen reminder.
Or yours may be a small part, which requires
that your light be extinguished—a firefly
no one will feel the lack of in that jigging chorus—
so that the perfection of the dream may be fulfilled.

Stay where you are, says that dream, you cannot do otherwise,
Try: you can't move your feet, can you? you
can't open your eyes.
You are mine.
I will deliver you
to where you are going.

No! the fear is your friend!
That sense of surrendering, being lifted up—it's not to a sky,
            but to nothing.
Believe you are right
to flee that dream,
frightened, perhaps in time, by the nightingale,
the song, the beautiful telltale song.
If it could, that song would scream, Run!

Run through the gate into the dark
that no one has dreamt yet,
to scramble in panic over the rooftops
lit only by stars.
You may yet escape; there is more than one of you,
and there may be others, later on,
friends you will meet in the dark.
Maybe you still can
outrun, or outwit, or change the terrible ending of
your civilization's dream.

After Bosch

To cure folly, cut open his head
And remove
Something.
The onlookers however
Appear pessimistic, and even the surgeon
Meticulous rather than hopeful.

Landscape by Poussin

after Landscape of St. Matthew and the Angel *in Berlin*

The sky is not very large, but it is blue,
With white clouds standing in it
As if they had been there for some time—
Standing, also, in the sense of "a standing appointment".
Nonetheless, this does not look like the day
To be setting out on a new adventure.
The two buildings visible here, one near, one far,
Are both ruins, the nearer one wholly dismembered.
For the rest, there is nothing at all spectacular
In this view, though the painter is said to have liked it.

The other colors blend—some of the dun earth's brown
Seems to have seeped upward into the trees.
The river's clay banks are high but level
As it winds, whitish grey and broadly reversing itself, into distance
But then rounds a bend and is lost between bluffs.
Waters are calm, solids are heavy and edged,
Things have come to rest.

This chapter has been written
Long ago, although you may be reading it only now,
And the book of which it is only a part
Has reached, it also, its final sentence.
The end of the story is known,
Though not yet by you, since you are still reading.
But if you look at this picture,
This landscape, this gravitational pull,
The story's direction will not escape you,
Nor you it.

You are not only a reader but a character in this story.
I give you, says the painter, what I have been given—
A glimpse of the last page.
It may come to you as a comfort, or it may not,
But you can cease to struggle.

Die Quelle zu dem Juengling (Franz Schubert)

I don't know what I say, and neither
did you, but it was said: flowed
and stayed. To tread the road of the sky
and then come back
where the brown leaves scatter across the earth
and springs congeal—
one doesn't last long so.
You died at thirty-one.
Water is too beautiful and too profound.
What the fountain drowses
is not for words.

That music
is the soft trace, as snow falls into the river,
of your recent appearance;
a footprint in the air.
The birds wing close to it, glinting past
evening, past morning's
crystalline desire.
In some very flowing,
rapid and changing direction often,
you knew; in midflow you knew three ways at once
of getting there, and took them all.

Gothic

In the great Gothic abbey of Fécamp,
its lofty church, pigeons
swoop, set off
echoes with their
peremptory applause.
Though the windows are glazed
with clear glass. What
cannot be contained, nor yet shut out.

Postscript to a Poem by John Ashbery

Dromedaries overtook me
As I was crossing the State Line
To get lost.
My underwear
Full of potato chips
That crumbled as I walked
Very irritating.

I stopped.
The dromedaries trundled by
Far too consequentially to be believed.
Nodding.

The Offering

(*Giovanni Bellini, nearing 90, paints*
The Drunkness of Noah*)*

Here in the vine-green, vine-bronze half light
the offering lies—the body, white like a child's,
and asleep.

Its substance is spent, the skin loose and soft
as a sack from which gold grain has steadily
poured until it is gone,
but a film of bright dust remains.
Its substance is spent, its light is not quenched.

The grapes have been gathered and pressed,
the wine has been poured and drunk.
A little lies darkly pooled
at the bottom of the bone-white cup.
The body sleeps, not as a child's: sleeps
after: after the fierce unsteady joy,
after the unforeseen weakness, after
the disappearance of years, a sleep
weighted by what, though forgotten,
has been known.

Above it circle the three celebrants, the sons
of the house, for whom the offering is made.
One laughs, haloed in vine leaves and shadow,
his teeth gleaming. One gazes, stupid and sorrowful.
One begins reverently to fold away
what should no longer be seen.
All three are needed.

Harvest and knowledge and vessel
are this body, my own, the offering
I have made.
What I am, what I know, I set down here.
At the end there is sleep
And there is light.

Mozart's Coronation Concerto

The string of pearls
An elegant fish line tautening
As something tugs, tugs
From below the shining surface

The sun glitters, the air is clear.
The bridge arcs onward, now
High
Above the channel

Then the heart-
Stopping lacunae, two
of them –swiftly spanned
but daringly; this
close to death one no longer needs
to worry about the
supports.

Piero della Francesca

Geometries—
Mathematical relationships—

When all that is mortal has died
When all that is material has
Disintegrated

Do these remain?
Remain, though invisible
In the white uninterrupted light that is
Eternity?

Triangles, circles,
Pyramids, spheres, cones: all
Perfect, the things of this world perfected:

Do they exist only in the minds of men
And die with us?

Or do they immutably furnish that vast room,
The mind of God, that widens into forever,
At which we may peer until our sight fails
Through the keyhole of a door
That remains always locked?

I shall never know.

Monet's Spring

Pink and grey, faint blue and vivid green
Wind and shadow hurrying through
The new grass, the still-bare budding trees
—a tide rushing in towards summer.

A summer now long past. The eyes that saw it
Perished, yet here it is,
About to be; here, now
Still to come.

The Limitations of Art

Bracelets unclasp; bridges unspan the river.
Vermeer tries to portray Hamlet, but without success.
Hamlet: his favorite play, in a spirited Dutch translation.

(Hamlet asleep, head cradled on hand, an overturned wineglass
On the table beside him; no; try again.
Hamlet seated at a table across from Ophelia
Who holds a wineglass, light streaming in
Irresistibly from the window at left, igniting
The room's white walls and everything
Within them—no; that's not the point, is it.
Hamlet standing, dressed in sky blue, reading
A letter, his mouth slightly open, a map
On the wall behind him—the North Sea? England?
Closer; but really, this isn't going to work.
It's not a good fit. Perfect though these
Pictures might be, they don't catch the essence.
Dammit!
Hamlet pouring milk in the kitchen….)

Wednesday

Up, or down, in the foothills of poetry,
the foothills of revelation, every day
is Wednesday, simple ways, and the end
of the week is never. Roots,
routines, mind cave-ins, and,
glimpsed through the interstices and curiously
everywhere but glimpsed usually
while just disappearing
behind something, or turning
purposefully out of town,
revelation.

Far away or deep within
or right there
again gone
again.

No day is the same.

There was a tree; it's gone now—

The smell of baking bread, maybe the bread
of life,
maybe just tomorrow's bread
and tomorrow, despite
what you might expect,
is Wednesday.

Venice Beach Fishing Pier

On the other hand, there is the fishing pier
At Venice Beach, on a clear blue weekend morning.
Looking out, the vast sea buckling slightly,
Forming gentle slides; looking back, at a distance
The cresting waves pouring over themselves, leisurely and powerful,
Sending back a thin shawl of bright spray from their shoulders.
Beyond, the broad sand, a long gaggle of squared-off houses
Like children's blocks, the invisible big city and
Several rows of mountains giving off a pale and pebbly sparkle
Jag the horizon. And, sashaying up the middle
On the stilted concrete pier, see all the people!
Here they come and there they go, fisher kings
And queens, old guys, young guys, middle aged
Ladies, jogging and running, dancing and standing still,
Walking their dogs and feeding a fish to the pelican,
All soaking up the bright, vast, vivid day,
The morning still early, and who knows what it will bring?

V

A Question About Insurance

An old style business street, brick walled and cobble floored;
A sign: Sun Fire Insurance Co.
These seem and are
Humdrum enough. Yet once
Were blots   blots of fire
Spreading and pulsing in void.
Then, after, fire
Shawled in strange substance,
Hooded. An elementary light
By slow degrees cooled, quarried, and begrimed
To be this hard featured street
In North Philadelphia.

O brightness of the immortal face
Which has become another, such an other
Place!

If things so strange can be
How then insure
Against the end, or the eventual shape,

Of anything?

Reflection from Middle Air

This is
autumn morning
the etched picture, a
phrase written in gray ink
the towers rising
losing themselves in
cloud
their faces becoming
vaguer, more
forgetful
southward the towers
of work, northward
cloud-neighboring houses
the economic structure
the social structure
these layered habitats
mean (forget)
lives
posited
high off the
ground (which is paved)
mean growing up and growing old,
loving and dying somewhere between
(the earth and the sky)
in glass-fronted shelves
mean
(forget
not yet)
slotted
lives.
Is that already the clock striking?

Waiting Area Gate C 3 LaGuardia Airport

Practice contemplation of the eternal
in an air swirling with very specifically time-bound
injunctions: e.g.
if you wish to visit Toronto
NOW is the time ("Groups 1, 2, 3, 4 boarding at Gate C 42")
RIGHT NOW and the same goes for
Oklahoma City, likewise Miami.

The eternal can wait. It's known
For being good at that. It can outwait you
without lifting a finger or
batting an eyelash.

So take off, if you will, for
the semi-arid and oil-spouting Southwest,
or the steamy alligator-infested Southeast,
or the upright and uptight North
(for a different view of this, however, see
the recent activities of Toronto's mayor.
they suggest that times have changed
In Toronto.)

Meanwhile, eternity continues
to wait.

Dead Poet

Not much good at parties,
you left long ago. Vanished. Buried in Camden
or some place like that.
Ceased to exist.
By few missed. But strangely
your circle of intimates has expanded to thousands
possibly going on millions.

And if we step outdoors after a cloudless sunset
and perhaps one or two subsequent drinks,
we may be able to see you climbing
up the night sky,
star by star by star.

If You Had Known

Soldier,
If you had known
that you were going to that far country
tomorrow,
would you have done otherwise?

But nobody believes.
We know that we are traveling, but
we do not expect to arrive.
Who could believe
that the far country
is not far, is now
less than a day's journey,
and that before tomorrow afternoon
you will cross the nonexistent border
without knowing
that you have done so?

You would have done otherwise.

Paper

Who dares say "clean"?
I need no lessons in Honesty
is the best—set afire
the republic. Refuse
amnesty.

How quiet tonight.
They have no voice.
Who are the defenseless?
They are unrecognizable.
Where are they now?
They are right here.
They are the trees cut down
to make paper
to print on
for the instruction of the still
unwilling to become paper
to print on, to read, and
to throw away.

Armadillo

Armadillo, little
armado, dust-pig turtle,
with your elegant silver feet and paternal mustache

Not to you will happen
what happens to other armed men.

Your dreams are not
of things higher than the life
that is yours now.

Glory and sacrifice
cut no dust with you

And if you are eaten alive
it is not by disgust,
not from within.

The Color of Your Money: A Story

We're talking about (set against
the gunmetal shrug, cosmic brood of grey skies)
the bright warm reds of money—
more fun than blood-red any day (just as
fire insurance is more fun than being in a fire)
and what the story is all about.
It's imaginary, like all the best stories, and therefore
you don't have to worry about the real loss of blood
or real death, or local lives that have much in common
with death -- it's all out there somewhere
else, but you can control life through that story,
if you are the storyteller you can ensure that your own life
never touches the ground
or even the pavement, rolls along on wheels,
takes place in air-conditioned interiors,
need not concern itself
with the other lives that lack those magical colors:
lives that the story also determines, but never mentions.

Menaces to Society and to the Planet

Persons perilous, you say—
adrift, shabby,
scraping the bottom
of the streets
in the dampshine
under the streetlights

shuffling an aimless
dance that always returns
to the same point;
folded up on the sidewalk

or climbing the rooming house
stairs askew
with stops to re-gather
breath or balance

Are these really the dangerous ones?
Are these the ones that could
and maybe will
destroy the world?

You, in your pride and power and control
Of events, might wish to consider more deeply
Your answer to this question.

Is This Aulis?

The muse has something to say: I
Will dictate to you the confession
Of the northwest wind.

It has tried, and successfully, to escape unseen
But it cannot pass unheard, and I never forget
A voice.

Is this Aulis? the ships are gone
and the white sky empty of omens.
Nothing is here but the salt-beds
the small square crusty beds that dry over
white, and the sky, and high up the slow hawk turning,
turning, turning
with a flash on the wind.

I am that wind.
They sold her unopened life to pay for me.
I was not consulted, but I came.
The ships piled up, piled up on the far shore.
The strangers killed and were killed.
Troy's flames blew east.

I cannot stop

Aulis, the port in which Agamemnon's daughter
Iphigenia was sacrificed to bring the wind that would
take his fleet to Troy

Money

Caramel calls from the far shore
Glittering blue as daisies
Of which no man, no lifetime can speak
With the authority of
Money.

Derrida doesn't detect
With the infallibility of
Money.

Poetry's seedy hotel rooms
Can only be rented with soft, pillowy
Money.

Heidegger is deeply concerned with being,
Which in many circumstances
And in our society's recorded announcement
Equates with
Money.

Don't let's talk about transumptions.
Silence is friendship in such a case.
Rather, nitric and indestructible,
Money.

The nacreous fog of tenderness is in the end
An illusion, liable to lift.
Theory too can vanish leaving no trace,
Leaving us clueless.
So if theory is to be expounded, let it be
The theory of
Money.

Blood, salt, stone, flies, sand, bone.
All these are nothing,
Make no never mind,
To money.

Newspaper Photo (Abu Ghraib)

She smiles winsomely up at the camera
Teeth gleaming, a ringlet lying
Coquettishly along her forehead—from where she crouches
Next to a battered-looking man packed in ice.
A pretty girl. Specialist Sabrina Harmon,
The caption tells us. It does not say
What her specialty is. But clearly
She has no knowledge of the meaning of ice.
In this context.
Its cold arrest.
She's in something pink; her aqua-gloved hand
Almost touches the rigid, ice-hard shoulder.
Too close, you might think, for comfort,
But seemingly no.
A smiling pretty girl. He
Is less prepossessing, his mouth open,
His eyes covered with what could be
White bandages or chips of ice, his
Brownish, stubbled cheek and jaw looking
Scuffed, like a worn shoe.

A pretty girl.

She is not aware
Of what until recently she shared
With this man, nor of what she still
Shares, and will
Share.
What lies in wait for her around a near
Corner. Her later life.
Nor that she too is subject to that cold arrest.

Fetish (Public Figure)

Man made in a
Doll's image, worth focusing on
Even by the restless eye
Because what you don't know
Can hurt you, but don't look
Too long

If you believe
Or if you cannot believe
Never meddle
With the dried flower
Arrangement, it may take you in,
Enlist you with its dragonfly claws
Into its lifeless jungle.

The doll is a false witness.
The image has a heart of stone.

The Drone

Not a pretty sight—
like a blind, winged catfish
—the snub nose, the blunt chin, the sullen
luster—as it weaves above the rippled sand,
the harsh dry mountains on its way to
a planned destination. But
it was not made for delight.

And not a gallant thought—
only the latest human device
for distributing death without danger
to the distributor—no valor called for,
the unexpected death sent now from so far
that nobody knows who the sender is, maybe
not even the sender.

And if it wander
by human error into a wedding party
or detonate sleeping children, well,
that was no one's intention.

Second Sunday in Advent

John the Baptist

If I could return,
Knowing what I now know,
Would I talk as much to you comfortable people
About the wrath to come?

No wrath to come is different
From the wrath that has been, wrath
Is wrath, and you seem to know so little
About the wrath that is.

Despite much evidence.
And the wilderness I would leave to
Shift for itself; if I preached there, no one
Would come to hear me. No,

I would come to you
In your cushioned pews in
Your snug-heated churches, where this morning you laugh
                    just a touch in excess
At the preacher's moderate jokes—

All in a spirit
Of good will, you are not really
Amused, nor moved, and your preachers do not expect
Nor intend you to be.

What could I tell you to your discomfort?

Shall I tell you that your warfare
Really is almost accomplished? That your day of
Death by proxy is passing, is
Nearly past?

What will you do without it?
How will you fatten without a wrath to come?

Shall I tell you, you that flatter yourselves
That God is made in your image,
That your imaged world, your galaxy, your universe
Is irredeemably silly?

That laughter—gusty,
Helpless, painful laughter is what befits it?
That no true prophet could keep himself, doubled over, from
Rolling in your aisles?

Irredeemable is a strong word,
Not for me to say. But I tell you
That even He who comes after may be able to do little
With the world you have made.

Oh generations of sleek, foolish,
Loveable, almost-well-intentioned
Vipers. With God, you will tell me,
All things are possible. You have seen it written.
And I tell you,
Don't count on it.

VI

Absence

I said I was not afraid of after
death, but I am. The absence.

Say what they will of grace,
epiphany, rejoining, I fear

the sealed black oblong under ground,
the concrete curtains, all barriers
made lasting.

Not-to-hear the jay's wild metal
call through all the forests and
suburbs and
graveyards of this continent
age after age, speaking
of no solution.

Not-to-know, as the roots twine on
and the leaves and the waters
whisper on and on,
that I'm forgotten.

At the Gates

Despite the notwithstanding
We welcome you, we as representatives
Of the order, an order of which you
Are as yet unaware: elusive,
Inescapable. Wings, yes, in a sense,
We have—you were not wrong about that
When you imagined us. But none of us hold
A sword, or scales.

And do not be afraid,
Do not be ashamed,
The dead are innocent
Now, whatever they once were.

If there were saved, if there were damned,
It was in their lives.
Your lives.

Look back:
The long plume of white smoke
Speaks you clean
As you always wanted to be.

Old 78

The record goes round and round and because it has gone round
Too often, the music I love is fibrous and partly lost
In the hiss and crumble of shellac.
It has become a record almost equally
Of the music and of abrasion.
The grooves are worn, and their circles grow smaller
Like ripples in the surface of a pond
Moving now not outward from but inward to
The original stone.

Perspective

It grows always clearer, that landscape:
Always clearer with distance, that landscape towards which you long,
Where you once were.
You see it
Rich and distinct in the morning light
As you gaze past a nondescript middle distance
And the blurred near objects that get in the way.
That landscape does not exist, has not
Now for a very long time.
But you journey towards it all the same
As it gets farther away, and clearer.

Bouquet River, West Branch

High, cool summer
the rock-slide white up on Giant Mountain
sun glittering over the silver meridian
smaller and smaller, a diamond chip
water glittering over stone
over the orange, putty color, white-blue
over and past
and never past

Beings live in that cold wrinkle of dazzle
stand flickering for an instant
against the flow of
their dense clear air
that like time
slants only one way

The watcher becomes
the watch-crystal
sun shines uninterrupted through
the irrelevant molecules of
a body that is
less than here

Man casts no shadow

Family Photographs

Very gently, so gentle in its descent
like the leaves drifting down
in random scythe patterns,
flickering yellow

Swinging down
through the calm air
with the quiet motion of pendulums

Faces strangely smiling upward
squinting into the sun
as they did on that day, many years past,
and, on paper, do still—

Floating, tilting, sinking
to their eventual, unplanned destination
where they lie with the others
covering the ground.

And oh, the sleep
for which leaves are the coverlet,
the sleep that has overtaken them all.

I Once Heard Her

"I want," she said, I once heard her remembering
"A little white house."
And it is little, the rooms so low,
One must stoop to enter.
"Where I can have all the people I love
Around me." And we shall all come,
In time, from the stranger places—
Out of the sea, from under the eucalyptus where I was resting,
From silver-sunned morning, from yellow-lit evening, from
The long, long and slumberous afternoons—smelling of salt,
Of camphor, of pine, not as we used to,
Nevertheless we shall be there, as close as, closer
Than we once were
In the house of weeping,
The house of song.

Te decet hymnus

"I want," she said, singing,
A little white horse,
Blind. Who knows without seeing,
Now it is night, the way to those places
I had forgotten.
And in them I'll dance
With the truth, my partner,
While fireworks go off on the lawn outside
Flash, boom! like a siege
And the stars ride higher,
Higher and higher,
Too high to see.

Autumn

Listen, it has something to tell you
in voices that sing to more than one sense,
autumn.

Not like what went before,
in the voice of the cicada's legs
and the sun's brass gong
—a long, nervous, big song
acrid all the day long.

Autumn and later autumn, in other voices'
darker and older tone:
the scutter of the crisp leaves
the wind
the deep earth hardening
the grey, wind-ribbed water
the colors moving toward brown
speaking in fugue
of the immense order
of forgetfulness.

In order to be again, you must forget what you were.

Magic

Home: sunrise and sunset were
    the first day
And in between came
    lunch

Lamb-and-barley soup, Mother bending down
    to take
Something out of the oven,
    her hands

Magic-carpeted with potholders
    a sweet-sour
Look preoccupying her
    mysterious familiar

Face. Her dust-colored hair hung
    over her ears.
She'd push it back when we sat down
    at table.

After supper Dad might tell our long
    continued story
About potions and turning to stone,
    the evil

Enchantress seen in the sky, a dark
    constellation
Headed our way, you'd hear
    her laugh

Just when you thought you were
    safe; or
Her friend, the magician who'd
    change

To a spider and weave an immense
    mist-colored
Web, so sticky, so strong
    that if

Once you touched it, even just
    touched it,
It had you. You'd never
    let go.

But our heroes always outfoxed them
    some way, except
When we were sent to bed
    in disgrace,

No story, for something we'd done we knew
    we shouldn't.
So they said. But we didn't
    see it that way.

We didn't expect it, and we still
    don't see it well,
That web. That everything is--
    each thing,

Each what happened, what will, is
    a consequence:
The soup bowl, the salt shaker on the
    wooden table,

The bending woman, the particulars of
    her gesture,
Tomorrow's escape, yesterday's,
    the oblong

Window, the light shining
    through it
Was, is, will be a connecting
    part,

A strand in what is so dense
      and fine
That no story can do more than
      allude to it:

What binds and cradles here, now—
      the web
Of will, chance, circumstance
      reaching

In multiple dimensions outward from
      or inward to
What we can't see
      at all.

Party on the Terrace

Nobody invited the skeleton bride,
But she came anyway, clicking and clacking
Beneath her veil in an off-putting
Fandango rhythm and trailing her
Train, by now rather ratty
Tat-tatty behind her like a tail.
Still, good smells came from the kitchen
Where she busied herself, and
Most of the guests were on the terrace
With their martinis, so hardly noticed.
Now and then someone would fall over
Into the canyons (we have a corner apartment).
Remind me to have someone in
To raise the railing; we've lost too
Many friends lately, especially tall ones, and with
Increasing frequency as the evening
Wears on. But everything has its downside,
And the view is good from the 83rd floor.
Wide horizons, and if you look straight down
The traffic looks like beetles and the people
Look like ants --- worker ants
Though I'm told some of them are currently
Unemployed. Oh; leaving already: Oh,
You aren't? All right, but could you
Tone down the fandango a bit?
It's upsetting some of our tall, fit friends,
You see? There goes another one.

Neversummer

This unnatural time, the hunter's season
And the dinosaur's, the short-breathed ghost
Of the dead summer. It does not appear every year, and then
For only a few days, blue grey and opaque,
When the leaves are gone but it is warm,
Too warm for the scum of ice on the ponds
To be believed.
The air is a broth, of more substance
Than the trees that inhabit it
Like delicate, ubiquitous dinosaur skeletons.
They let in light unexpectedly throughout.
At night, which comes early, their branches
Devolve still further into vapor
While the moon shines
And at a distance the cold-skinned lakes
Gleam dully like flagstones.

In the upstairs bedroom, a sound from before:
The sizzling of a leftover fly
At the window, called back from its flawless sleep
To a world from which flies
Have been forgotten.
The room is possessed by its furious sizzle
Punctured by
Little clicks and thumps
As of an impatient thimble.

I am also called back: to the hand.
Squarish, like mine; a little puffy and spotted, and when
I last touched it, unfamiliarly grained. The skin
Had become very shallow and
It clothed only cold.
The philosopher hand which had forgotten
That it once knew,
Had become simple,
Unlearned itself
To an aggregate
Of conoid forms.

To My Father, on His 101st Birthday

(nothing of him doth remain
but hath suffered a sea-change
into something rich and strange)

Full fathom five, father.
No coral, no pearls:
Transmuted flesh—but still with bones, blood, nerves.
Strange change indeed.
It can be felt to grow.
And what remains of you
Is us—six other
People: two boys and a girl,
Then two girls and a boy.

Strange change, but yes,
It is rich.   And it is you, though
Less concentrate, diffused and mixed
Like mineral currents in the
Salt sea you once loved, swam in, sailed upon,
And in whose ships you travelled.

Take comfort yet.
For what happened then is not over.
You are not drowned.

The Dream

When I was twelve years old I dreamed one terrible night
That I was myself, no different
From how I always was, and so was our house
and the maple tree in front and the yard
and the road beyond. I'd just come out, and
I went to the tree, I wanted
To swing round it, sort of, pretending
I was going to Italy—it was too big to really
Swing around, and I was too big
To really pretend.
But I put my hand on its trunk and started
Around, feeling its rough bole rotate under my hand
Like the turning earth.
When I had gone half round and was coming back
To where I had been, the blue sky
Dazzled; I knew something was wrong.
I ran back in. Where my grandmother had been sitting
There was nothing, no chair, the room
Tall, quiet, and empty.
From the back of the house my baby sister called, her voice clear
As a ray of prismed light. From somewhere nearer by
My mother answered. Her voice was sheathed in rust.
Then the house was still again, so still
That I could hear out of the distance
The long-continued voice of the train at night
Rolling along its rails
And the quiet breath
Of my wife in the bed beside me.

7th Floor at 84

Balcony—
Iron railing waist high;
Repeating, retreating silvery clouds,
their violet undersides—into the distance
beyond the railing—
Closer by tree tops' faded red
nearer still the inviting, treacherous air—
because once launched, you couldn't change your mind
and not do it after all,
because then it would be
after
all.

Pouring a Child's Glass of Milk

Refrigerator door closes "cloop."
I start to tilt the carton to dispense
Some bovine mother's milk, and think

Calcium.
Something very important.
Inanimate, insensible, but
Like us at our sexy best
Voracious to merge and make
An unpredictable new self beyond itself.

Now I pour the
Smooth white like thinned white paint, watch
Its quick, velvet-grooved, arrowy flow
While the glass
Makes the sound of a glass filling up

And I think what that liquid will become,
Will build out of crystals to become,
Becoming jointed, and how long
It will last,

How long outlast
What it supported, what had pulsed
And stretched around it
Back then, in a time
Now still to come.

Penmanship: Storage

Foreigners, ikons, something from far away—
Or right here,
These symbols show, that I was taught as a child
In the second, third, fourth grades
Under Miss Brooks, Miss Clough, Miss Morin
Who knew no more than I did of
What this was for, what it
Could mean, how other peoples' lives
Two thousand years ago, or four,
Could be stored here --- along with theirs,
Their own tender possessions

—And mine.
(And after all, Miss Brooks,
Miss Clough, probably even beautiful red-gold-haired Miss Morin
Are dead now --- all that's left,
What they taught, what they had learned)
Those symbols: the flow of ink
Taking certain forms; standing in for
The flow of blood in millions of human beings,
Telling us what life was. What life is.

Douglas Firs, Old Growth

Male and female he did not create them
But both at once,
nor did he grant them
The power of speech, though they give voice
To the wind,
nor the power of motion, except
Up.
But in their case, what an exception!

They stand for eight hundred years "rooted
(In our phrase) to the spot,"—with astonishment?
What can our kind of consciousness know
Of theirs?
Do they grasp contentment in earth? Feel
The deep pleasure of thirst quenched
In water as it rises through their cells? Find
Rapture in light or in the intermingling
With air? Do they suffer fire? How
Do they know, these immense and stately intelligences?
These bodies that unfurl and mount and ramify
Hugely through slow time?

This one, for instance, began its climb,
Its leisurely vast arising,
About when the Gothic builders
Started to look at its cousins and say
" I can do that too " in stone.
Wonderful works, records and proofs of mind
In which, like this living wood, stones dance
At heights beyond any tightrope
Stationary leaps and twists and spirals
That go on for hundreds of years.

Those spires we can love and be mazed by because
Our kind made them. These, because
What they record, whatever they prove,
It isn't us.
We're strategists, our lives
A quick-breathed, quick-spent sprint
For survival, and we pass survival on
In a few moments of ecstasy. What their ecstasy may be
Is not ours to know. Their lives breathe
Differently, and their long race
Is in standing still—
Their long, long race towards the sun.
They stand
Intricate and living in the blue afternoon,
Impassible, yet seeming benign.

Hidden Costs

Invisible TV – now there's a thought!
Hearty subdivisions guffaw and reach for the remote,
Soignée suburbs surreptitiously titter and tune in
With a sigh of relief. Now we can be tuned in
Without having to look at anything; tuned in
And tuned out at the same time.
Or was that always the case?

O rectangular technicolor eye cornering the globe,
    motormouth marketeer,
Don't talk to me about tangerines you don't mean.
I'm not interested in the ambient sneeze
As brokered by Merck Medco
Nor in your cheery retailing, while spokespersons lick their chops,
Of the disasters you help bring about.

No wonder we turn ugly as you watch – beautiful humanity turns
Ugly and varnished and heartless.

Beauty is in the eye of the beholder.

The Instrument

A shape of breath;
A ladder for sound, whose detachable rungs
Are fingers; an old thought articulate in
A new, wood throat.

The thought is wondering Haydn's, the breath
Is mine, but no human cry only
Is so pure.
This is the voice of the pear tree
Which did not know that it lived.

Ecstasy: Major, Minor, and Otherwise

Ecstasy
Like a fish darting olive-brown through water
Then turning sideways into the sun with a
Flash
blind Silver
Knocking you back.
That's one kind.

And how do we carry each other?
From newlywed day on
Through nights and days and years?

Hands snoozing the kitchen table then
Finding each other, or finding
Each other's knees. Smiles finding
Each other, minds
Finding each other from opposite sides
Of a largish room.
Those strange unpredictable
Plunges quick or slow
To be continued
Into what we don't know,
But know.

That's another.

Heaven

Heaven: was it always a sales pitch?
Certainly, whether or not, it worked, and still works
For many of us. But,

There's that blue. Translucent
As it appears, transparent as it is, it might as well be
Opaque. We can't see through it;

That is, we can see through it, even fly through it
But though it's as clear as nothing we can't see through it
To whatever lies beyond.

It remains blue. And yet,
Not flat, not shallow; deep; the eye
Gets lost in it. Rapture—a continuous rapture.

So: maybe home, but an enigmatic home.
And home was the essence of it—of folk heaven
As an idea. Reunion. Coming back

To find the people we loved, all there,
And all unchanged, but with no more cause for quarrel,
Neither in them nor in us.

On the Escalator at the Seattle Convention Center

Light floods in through the huge wall-window.
I pause at the top
And watch artists and art historians
Borne effortlessly up the long, gleaming diagonal
As if on trays, foreshortened bodies and upturned faces
Mostly anxious, or preoccupied, or calculating;
I step carefully on, to begin my unhurried parallel descent

And there you are—
At a stage in your life well before I met you
Your hair still straw-blonde
With skeins of deeper gold,
Your long body taut; you're smiling,
Your face an almost transparent vessel
Of eagerness, of delight looked-for,
Its glass not yet etched, or bleared, or darkened.
The light shines through.

Me, of course, you don't recognize.
You haven't met me yet, won't for some years,
And do not notice me as we pass.

I think of the other you, the one I know
But don't see any more; tall and long-legged, like you.
When we met, she older than I,
Her hair was already prematurely white, but vivid,
Like the flash of her smile, easy and ardent.

Now, I'm told, almost a recluse,
She sits brittle-boned in her New York apartment.
The jazzy one-time girl, the frightened old lady.
I wonder,
How much does it matter? Since it is so.

It matters to her, and to a few
She loved, those still alive. But
If venturesome light still sparkles, still finds a vessel,
A housing, how much does it matter?
Tell me: is the last state more than the first
Just because it comes after?

Point of Departure, Many Years After

But there's more, Hegel is not the winner,
Though Goya may be. Destiny
Is seen to be less mild than you'd thought.
The tide turns, the waiting sand
Fills up, begins to mirror in blurry iridescence
You where you stand. Your solid shadow
Films over with water.
The wharf, landlocked in blackberries,
Is unreachable. It's been that long.

Sound, Heard Long Ago from Behind a Closed Door at the Old People's Home

A long, impersonal moan, might make one think of a
Very large water-bird, bigger than a gull
And lower-voiced. Or a ferry's horn in the middle distance.
Or the empty wind, blowing through something or past something.
A straight sound, no variation, no syllable, no inflection.
Again, with no variation, no syllable, no inflection.
Again.
Yet the sound has in it something of grief.
Of captivity. Of time's insane collapse.
Of gulls swerving vainly against the wind.

Walking the Dog This Autumn

Missing . . .

(a sign glued to a telephone pole;
somebody's
loved creature)

Missing. . . .

I watch a golden leaf-boat
float down a clear stream,
spin slowly, continue on

And remember watching
the same thing happen
sixty-five years ago
when I was seven,
bemused and delighted.

Missing . . .

(an extra dimension)

More leaves (more
golden boats)
fan out from the trees
on a light wind.

One
circles my head, slants past my
shoulder, launches

With hardly a tremor
on the water.

Walking the Dog the Night Before Christmas Eve

A muddle of sky and cloud,
Black branches, motionless, gesturing against them;
Minus motion, the gestures appear melodramatic, somewhat
Unconvincing. Underfoot,
The mushy crunch of snow.
Trainhoot through wet air.
All so familiar, so long accustomed.
Yet I still can't believe
They mean only what they are.

Nor Does It Matter

Nor does it matter
As you drown in the embrace
Of your last, your only finally faithful
Lover, that your body
Is cold against his,
Or if no wisp, no vestige of ocean dream
Fumes up in your skull:
To him it is the same
If you have come to him robed
In the gold and red of your youth
Or the silver and ivory of your old age.
And now it is the same to you also.
Your blue eyes are closed
As you founder still deeper.
You do not see his brown shoulders
Looming over you
Nor the spring of black hair
But perhaps you feel
The strength of the long arms that enclose you,
Of the fingers that sift through
That patchwork of what once was
Gorgeousness.

For
Though your body
When it went under was a hulk—
Time-battered, one breast missing,
Weathered and chipped and blurred
Like those stone women left over
From the pediment of the Parthenon
And now beached in a museum—
Still, like theirs, it was once
The body of a goddess
Who could not cease to be

Or cease to love. And it still is,
Since for him
What was and what is are one,
The one that is none.
And now for you also.

Sleep then, clasped. upheld,
In that long, that deep embrace,
Sleep (upheld and pulled under) clasped
          in the glow of fire, the clearness of air,
The swirl of water, the rich dark of earth,
Clasped in the one that is none,
The one that is all.

Words of Love

I.
Those words keep coming back
Like steps pacing a floor in an empty house
Though the people will never come back,
Never appear again
Through time's blue smoke
That hangs for a moment almost still
Among the nearly leafless trees, before
It stirs, lifts, thins, dissolves to let be seen
The clear-burning winter night
Where universes flame on, islands
Of fire in the void,
The cold of space.

When I was five, Miss Whitcomb
Was sixty-five, so old
As to be a wonder when I met her on the path,
Her flesh a brownish wrinkled curtain
Washed so thin that I could see
Always through it the white
Of eternity.

When I was twenty-five, the one
I thought I loved was young, solid and sweet
To touch and sight, we lived now, laughed, though
Her voice was rather tuneless, and
The words keep coming back
That we did not say
Laughing and talking

I remember the words without voice
And the voices with no words

I did not know then, nor did she,
That we spoke in farewell, she
Raising a hand as she retreats to beyond where
She can come back again, a gesture of the hand
Already indistinct.

Words, though, come back. The smoke thins and rises.
Footprints lose their heat.
The lungs that gave breath, that empowered
The word, they have ceased
To take in and give out, have ceased
Even to be.
The words keep coming back.
Though the flesh is consumed.

II.
Like love,
The moonlight lies lazily along the roof-slates
Salving and sealing, healing and annealing
—I cannot possibly tell you how—it
Descries the blues and within them the reds
And delicately, liquidly, with a silvery cool nearly-
Gold lets them be, lets them be seen, brings them into
A being more than they ever knew
They could be.
I to you, you to me.

Oh words of want
That were never spoken, oh worlds
Beyond our aching and dying selves—

Stars brilliantly sparkling in a night sky
Under which we haltingly speak—avow—
Do not vow, says the void,
Your love is as frail as your life, and as little
Within your power.
Yet we vow

And have been able to remain,
As our fires begin to diminish, burn
Still fierce but a little more
Like those distant stars,
Faithful
To the words we have spoken
And still speak.

Oh, love.

Made in the USA
Middletown, DE
20 February 2017